SALT & PEPPER

A Full-length Play

by

JOSE CRUZ GONZALEZ

Dramatic Publishing

Woodstock, Illinois • England • Australia • New Zealand

*** NOTICE ***

The amateur and stock acting rights to this work are controlled exclusively by THE DRAMATIC PUBLISHING COMPANY without whose permission in writing no performance of it may be given. Royalty must be paid every time a play is performed whether or not it is presented for profit and whether or not admission is charged. A play is performed any time it is acted before an audience. Current royalty rates, applications and restrictions may be found at our Web site: www.dramaticpublishing.com, or we may be contacted by mail at: DRAMATIC PUBLISHING COMPANY, P.O. Box 129, Woodstock IL 60098.

COPYRIGHT LAW GIVES THE AUTHOR OR THE AUTHOR'S AGENT THE EXCLUSIVE RIGHT TO MAKE COPIES. This law provides authors with a fair return for their creative efforts. Authors earn their living from the royalties they receive from book sales and from the performance of their work. Conscientious observance of copyright law is not only ethical, it encourages authors to continue their creative work. This work is fully protected by copyright. No alterations, deletions or substitutions may be made in the work without the prior written consent of the publisher. No part of this work may be reproduced or transmitted in any form or by any means, electronic or mechanical, including photocopy, recording, videotape, film, or any information storage and retrieval system, without permission in writing from the publisher. It may not be performed either by professionals or amateurs without payment of royalty. All rights, including, but not limited to, the professional, motion picture, radio, television, videotape, foreign language, tabloid, recitation, lecturing, publication and reading, are reserved.

For performance of any songs, music and recordings mentioned in this play which are in copyright, the permission of the copyright owners must be obtained or other songs and recordings in the public domain substituted.

© MMII by
JOSE CRUZ GONZALEZ

Printed in the United States of America
All Rights Reserved
(SALT & PEPPER)

ISBN: 1-58342-096-7

For Rubén Sierra

IMPORTANT BILLING AND CREDIT REQUIREMENTS

All producers of the play *must* give credit to the author(s) of the play in all programs distributed in connection with performances of the play and in all instances in which the title of the play appears for purposes of advertising, publicizing or otherwise exploiting the play and/or a production. The name of the author(s) *must* also appear on a separate line, on which no other name appears, immediately following the title, and *must* appear in size of type not less than fifty percent the size of the title type. Biographical information on the author(s), if included in the playbook, may be used in all programs. *In all programs this notice must appear:*

"Produced by special arrangement with
THE DRAMATIC PUBLISHING COMPANY of Woodstock, Illinois"

Salt & Pepper was first presented as a staged reading in June 2000, at the Kennedy Center, as part of New Visions/New Voices 2000.

Salt & Pepper was read at Childsplay's New Play Project on May 23, 2000 in Tempe, Arizona. The New Play Project was made possible in part by a generous grant from the Whiteman Family.

Salt & Pepper premiered at Childsplay on October 27 through November 19, 2000 at the Tempe Performing Arts Center, Tempe, Arizona. The production was directed by Graham Whitehead and including the following cast:

Hannah . . . . LISA RANDOLPH KINDALL
Andy. . . . . JERE LUISI
Salt . . . . GORDON WAGGONER
Old Man. . . . . JON GENTRY and D. SCOTT WITHERS
Pepper . . . . ANDREA MORALES

Production Staff and Crew

Set and Costume Design . . . . GRO JOHRE
Lighting Design . . . . PAUL BLACK
Sound Design . . . . JULIE RANDOLPH
Fight Choreography . . . . LARRY GRUBBS
Properties Master. . . . . PAMELA HOUSER
Stage Manager. . . . . SARAH TERNAN
Production Manager . . . . ANTHONY RUNFOLA
Technical Director. . . . . ANDREW CAMPBELL
Scenic Artist . . . . JOLANE MORGAN
Master Carpenter   DAVE EKHOLM
Costume Construction/Wardrobe Supervisor . . . .
                                            D. DANIEL HOLLINGSHEAD
Master Electrician . . . . TIM MONSON
Electrician . . . . CASSANDRA FLYNN

The world premiere production of *Salt & Pepper* was presented as part of the Whiteman Foundation New Plays Program. Significant additional funding came from the Flinn Foundation, COMPAS, the Children's Theatre Foundation and Boeing Employees Community Fund, and the Children's Theatre Foundation of America.

Special thanks to Dan O'Neill and Jenny Lucier, David Lucier/The Barnes House, David and Sonja Saar, Graham and Margaret Whitehead, Rosemary and Patrick Walsh, Debra K. Stevens, and Childsplay Resident Company and Staff, Palabras, Gordon Waggoner, and to my family, Cory, Casey and Kelsey.

SALT & PEPPER

A Full-length Play
For 3 Men and 2 Women

CHARACTERS

SALT . . a 10-year-old boy. Loves his grandpa and brother.

PEPPER . a 10-year-old Latina girl. She dresses like a boy. She likes to read books.

OLD MAN . Salt and Andy's grandfather. Hannah's father. In his 50s. He is a hard man to live with.

ANDY . . . . a 17-year-old boy. Salt's older brother. Very protective of Salt.

HANNAH . . . . . appears as a memory. She has a beautiful singing voice. She is Salt and Andy's mother.

SETTING: A small agricultural town, somewhere near a desert, 1952.

Approximate running time: 55 minutes

To the best of our knowledge, the children's songs: Hush 'n' Bye; Johnny Get Your Hair Cut (Hey Betty Martin); Built My Lady a Fine Brick House; Go to Sleepy Baby, Bye; and The Juniper Tree, which are used in this play, are considered public domain. Melody lines appear at the back of the playbook.

SALT & PEPPER

SCENE 1

SETTING: *Onstage are letters of the alphabet scattered about. They come in all different shapes and sizes. The letter characters are not in any recognizable order. They may be used to create settings as well as words.*

AT RISE: *HANNAH appears. There's a glow about her. HANNAH is a memory. She throws the small paper characters up into the air. She is a young woman. She wears a plain cotton dress. She wears no shoes.*

HANNAH *(singing)*.
Hush 'n' Bye
Don't you cry
Oh, you pretty little babies

When you wake
You'll get sweet cake
And all the pretty little ponies

A brown and a grey
And a black and a bay
All the pretty little ponies

OLD MAN *(offstage)*. Hannah?

9

(HANNAH runs and hides. The OLD MAN, Hannah's father, enters. He is half dressed in overalls and carries a lantern. He wears no shoes.)

OLD MAN. Hannah, where are you?

HANNAH. Hidin', Daddy! You gotta find me!

OLD MAN. Hannah, it's the middle of the night.

HANNAH. Where am I?

OLD MAN. You gonna catch yourself a cold.

HANNAH. It's been rainin' letters again.

OLD MAN. Letters?

HANNAH. In all shapes and sizes mixed together.

(HANNAH throws some letters into the air. She runs and hides again. The OLD MAN searches for her.)

OLD MAN. Where are you?

HANNAH. I've collected a bunch of 'em, see? Ain't it beautiful, Daddy?

(HANNAH throws some more letters into the air. She runs off again. The OLD MAN searches for her.)

OLD MAN. Honey, come inside where it's safe.

HANNAH. I can't, Daddy.

OLD MAN. Why not?

HANNAH. 'Cause I'm writin' you a postcard.

OLD MAN. A postcard?

HANNAH. Give up?

OLD MAN. No.

HANNAH. I found me the most pretty one you ever seen. Look! *(Her hand appears. She holds up a small post-card.)*

OLD MAN. There you are!

HANNAH. It's a picture of the Grand Ole Opry. Ain't it the most beautiful buildin' you ever seen? It's where I'm gonna make my professional debut.

OLD MAN. Debut? What's that?

HANNAH. It means I'm gonna sing in front of the whole world, Daddy. And you gonna be proud of me. People will want my autograph and want me to star in their Hollywood pictures!

OLD MAN. Let me see your forehead.

HANNAH. I ain't got a fever! *(She crosses away from him.)*

OLD MAN. You ain't makin' any sense, Hannah.

HANNAH. That's 'cause it's a dream, Daddy.

OLD MAN. A dream?

HANNAH. And it yours.

OLD MAN. Mine?

HANNAH. Yes, sir. Rememberin' how things were. Good and bad. But there isn't much time.

OLD MAN. Time for what?

HANNAH. Before I go away.

OLD MAN. Why you wanna do that?

HANNAH. It's in the postcard, Daddy. All you gotta do is read it.

OLD MAN. Hannah, you can't leave.

HANNAH. Daddy, I gotta go and find my future.

OLD MAN. But it's here with your boys and me.

HANNAH. It's in the wind callin' to me.

OLD MAN. What wind?

HANNAH. The same one that brings the rain and the duststorms. It's callin' my name…wantin' to sweep me up and take me far away.

OLD MAN. To where?

HANNAH. Anywhere my little songs will he heard, Daddy.

OLD MAN. There's nothin' but heartache out there. I seen it. Felt it.

HANNAH. That's all I've ever known, but not no more. I'm gonna let that wind carry me and my babies into the future and take us wherever it wants.

OLD MAN. But them boys are too little to go anywhere.

HANNAH. That's why I need your help, Daddy. You gotta come with me.

OLD MAN. I ain't goin' nowhere and neither are you.

HANNAH. If I don't go now I'll just wither away and die. Can't you understand?

OLD MAN. No, I can't. You got a place here. Ain't that enough?

HANNAH. I made up my mind.

OLD MAN. I forbid you to go!

HANNAH. I'm takin' my babies with me.

OLD MAN. No, you ain't. You wanna go chase after some stupid dream then go, but them boys are stayin' here with me.

HANNAH. No.

OLD MAN. You made your choice. So get!

HANNAH. Please, Daddy…

OLD MAN. Get off my place! Get! *(HANNAH rushes away dropping the postcard.)* Hannah?! Hannah?!

HANNAH *(singing)*.
    Hush 'n' Bye
    Don't you cry…

OLD MAN. Don't you leave!

HANNAH *(singing)*.
    Oh, you pretty little babies…

OLD MAN. Hannah!

(The OLD MAN stands there for a moment, alone. He sees the postcard lying on the ground. He picks it up, crumpling it and throwing it to the ground. A moment later he picks it up and places it in his pocket.)

SCENE 2

A country song is heard. ANDY, a 17-year-old boy, enters flipping a large blue pancake from a frying pan high into the air. He grabs a plate of multicolored pancakes stacked atop one another. SALT, Andy's younger brother, rushes in wearing a metal pot on his head and carrying a broom as weapon. He falls to the floor, shooting everything in sight.

SALT. Pa-pow! Pa-pow! Pa-pow! Pa-pa-pa-pa-pow! *(Enemy fire is returned at SALT.)* Ughhh!!! Pow! Ughhh! *(SALT's death is dramatic. He falls onto one of the letters. Beat. Opening his eyes:)* You wanna play war, Andy?
ANDY. No.

SALT. Come on! I'll be the enemy.

ANDY. Go away, Salt. Can't you see I'm busy?

SALT. Whatcha doin'?

ANDY. Makin' breakfast.

SALT. Pancakes?

ANDY. Yup.

SALT. Colored ones?

ANDY. Yup.

SALT. Which colors you makin'?

ANDY. I got green, yellow and blue. *(He flips the blue pancake high into the air and catches it with the plate of colored pancakes.)*

SALT. Wo! Can I help?

ANDY. Take that stupid pot off your head.

SALT. Andy, I can't do that.

ANDY. Why not?

SALT. 'Cause it's my helmet! It's my only protection.

ANDY. Against what?

SALT. The enemy. They're all around. Hidin'. Waitin' to strike me dead.

ANDY. Well, you look real stupid, Salt.

SALT. I ain't stupid!

ANDY. Fine, then you can't help!

SALT. Okay, there, see! *(He drops his helmet to the floor.)*

ANDY. Too late.

SALT. Andy!

ANDY. I guess there's nothin' to save you now!

SALT. Huh?

ANDY. From the hounds of war! *(He howls loudly and then sticks his arms out and flies by SALT making air-plane noises.)*

SALT. Air raid!

(SALT grabs the pot and puts it back on his head. ANDY returns, strafing SALT. SALT uses his broom as an anti-aircraft gun.)

ANDY. I'm hit!
SALT. Yeah!
ANDY. But now I'm a kamikaze!
SALT. Oh, no, duck for cover!
ANDY. Too late!

(ANDY crashes into SALT. SALT and ANDY lie there dead. Beat.)

SALT *(jumping up)*. I won!
ANDY. No you didn't! You're dead!
SALT. No, I'm not, see?! It was my general!
ANDY. What?!
SALT. You killed my general, but I still lived!
ANDY. Salt, nobody survives a kamikaze attack.
SALT. But I did! You lost! I won! Victory dance! *(He pounds out a beat on his helmet using wooden spoons. He dances a victory dance.)*
ANDY. Will you be quiet!
SALT. Sore loser.
ANDY. Salt, eat your pancakes!
SALT. They're gonna need more salt.
ANDY. I already added some. Eat.

(SALT grabs a blue pancake. He rolls it up and eats it.)

SALT. Um…blue one's real good!
ANDY. It don't taste any different from the others.

SALT. It do too. Blues taste different from yellows. Yellows taste different from greens. Greens taste real different from blues.

ANDY. Whatever you say, Salt…

SALT. Andy, who taught you how to make colored pancakes? Was it Ma?

ANDY. No.

SALT. Then who?

ANDY. I can't tell you that.

SALT. Why not?

ANDY. 'Cause it's a big fat secret.

SALT. But you can tell me. We're brothers. Right?

ANDY. Nope. We ain't brothers. Somebody left you on the porch step. The old man took you in 'cause all you did was cry.

SALT. That ain't true!

ANDY. Sure is!

SALT. Well, I don't care 'bout your big fat secret! I don't wanna know!

ANDY. Fine. Suit yourself. But you better hurry before the old man gets here. It's your turn to wash them plates.

SALT. I can't, my arms got broke.

ANDY. Salt!

SALT. They are. See? They won't move. *(He wiggles his body and his arms flap side to side.)*

ANDY. You ain't weaselin' outta this again. It's your turn.

SALT. No, I'm not gonna do 'em.

ANDY. Yes, you are! *(He grabs SALT in a headlock.)*

SALT. Ow! Let me go!

ANDY. Not until you say "I give."

SALT. Why do I always gotta wash 'em?

ANDY. When you learn how to cook then you won't have to do 'em! Now say it!

SALT. No!

ANDY. Say it!

SALT. I give!

(ANDY releases SALT. SALT places his helmet back on.)

ANDY. When the old man catches you wearin' that pot on your head, you're gonna be sorry.

SALT. No I won't.

ANDY. Why's that?

SALT. 'Cause he loves me more than you.

ANDY. Oh, really?

SALT. Yup. So you better watch out.

ANDY. He's been in a foul mood all week.

SALT. That's 'cause he wrecked his truck and hurt his arm.

ANDY. And he's takin' it out on me. It ain't no picnic.

OLD MAN *(offstage)*. Andy?

ANDY. See?

SALT. It's Grandpa!

(The OLD MAN enters. He wears overalls, boots, a soiled baseball cap and gloves. His arm is in a sling.)

OLD MAN. Salt, go get ready for school.

SALT. Yes, sir.

OLD MAN. And take that stupid pot off your head. *(To ANDY.)* Don't you hear me callin' you?

ANDY. No, sir.

OLD MAN. Well, we got a truck to fix. It ain't gonna fix itself.

ANDY. I was gonna eat first.

OLD MAN. The day already started.

ANDY. I'm hurryin'.

OLD MAN. You stayin' out nights don't help any.

ANDY. I got my reasons.

OLD MAN. Well, your reasons ain't helpin' me fix my truck. All that schoolin' you're so proud of, where's it got you? It can't fix my truck engine. And you know even less about produce. I got a business to run. Them bills ain't gonna pay themselves.

ANDY. All you ever do is complain.

OLD MAN. 'Cause you give reason.

ANDY. I'm gonna leave one day and then you'll be sorry.

OLD MAN. You'll never leave.

ANDY. I might. I got plans.

OLD MAN. Plans?

ANDY. I wanna see the world. Travel to faraway places. Learn to speak different languages even.

OLD MAN. How are you gonna do that?

ANDY. I'm gonna join the Marines.

OLD MAN. The Marines? They won't take you. You just like your ma. Head in the clouds. And look where it got her.

ANDY. I'm gonna show you.

OLD MAN. Well, you show me how to fix my truck first, 'cause while you're under my roof you'll do as I say! There ain't no room for fools or dreamers in this house.

ANDY. Fine, I'm goin'!

(ANDY storms out. The OLD MAN eats one of the colored pancakes.)

OLD MAN. Blue one's good. At least he learned how to cook.

(SALT enters combing his hair and dressed for school. He hums "Go to Sleepy Baby Bye.")

OLD MAN. What's that song you hummin', Salt?

SALT. I don't know.

OLD MAN. I heard it before.

SALT. Where?

OLD MAN. That was one of the songs your mama liked to sing.

SALT. Really?

OLD MAN. She had the prettiest voice you ever heard.

SALT. I don't remember her too good.

OLD MAN. She was always singin' and playin' her guitar for you boys. Wrote her own songs and even made records too. Just about everybody in Nashville knew her.

SALT. Andy says she had her own bus with her name written on it.

OLD MAN. Oh, that's right. She was a big radio star too. She was always singin' at the Grand Ole Opry and she even went to make a Hollywood picture once.

SALT. My ma was a movie star?

OLD MAN. I think she even won one of them actin' awards.

SALT. How come Ma didn't ever take us with her?

OLD MAN. Well, that's 'cause she was always on the road. Them entertainers have got a lot of travelin' to do and it ain't no place for little ones. That's why you two come to live with me.

SALT. Was Ma rich?

OLD MAN. She had so much money she had to put it in two banks.

SALT. No.

OLD MAN. Yup, but she gave it all away to needy people.

SALT. My ma was somethin' else, wasn't she?

OLD MAN. She loved you a whole lot.

SALT. Grandpa, did my ma go to school?

OLD MAN. For a little while 'til Andy was born.

SALT. She did real good for herself and she didn't need no school.

OLD MAN. That's right.

SALT. You know more about things than my teachers do.

OLD MAN. Well…

SALT. Why do I gotta go to school, Grandpa? Everythin' I need to know is right here with you. One day, I wanna drive a truck just like you.

OLD MAN. You do?

SALT. Ah huh.

OLD MAN. Well, maybe missin' one day won't hurt.

SALT. You mean I don't have to go?

OLD MAN. Nope.

SALT. I'll work real hard and I won't complain like Andy.

OLD MAN. Then go get changed. We got us a truck to fix and produce to deliver!

SCENE 3

A bus is heard driving away. HANNAH enters carrying her guitar and suitcase. An image of a postcard appears behind her.

HANNAH. Dear Daddy, I've ridden the wind and it's carried me as far as Hope, Texas. I ain't got a cent to my name but it don't matter. I'm writin' this postcard to tell you I'm doin' fine. I'm gonna send you a picture postcard from every place I go, so you'll know where I've been. I hope you'll show them to my babies and explain what I am doin'. I know you're still mad and I don't expect you'll write me, but that's okay. Well, I gotta go for now, Daddy. Yours truly, Hannah.

SCENE 4

The OLD MAN and ANDY enter carrying crates of produce. SALT drags one in.

OLD MAN. We ain't got all day, Andy!

ANDY. I'm workin' as fast as I can!

OLD MAN. A snail is faster than you!

ANDY. Well, I don't see one liftin' these heavy crates!

OLD MAN. If we don't get this produce off to market today, we ain't gettin' paid. We need the money. You see this?! *(He holds out a stack of bills.)*

SALT. What are they, Grandpa?

OLD MAN. They're bills. Lots of 'em.

ANDY. I didn't wreck the truck. You did.

OLD MAN. How was I suppose to know they was fixin' a road? There were no road signs.

ANDY. Yes, there were.

OLD MAN. You weren't even there to help. That's my point.

ANDY. Well, what do you want me do?

OLD MAN. Tell me what they say. I ain't got my glasses.

SALT. I'll help you, Grandpa.

OLD MAN. No, I need Andy to do it, Salt. It's his job. He goes into town and pays the bills. 'Cept lately his head's been somewhere else and he ain't been no good for nothin'. Well, how much do I owe? *(He removes a roll of dollar bills held together by a rubber band.)*

ANDY. This one's five dollars!

OLD MAN *(counting)*. One, two, three—

ANDY. This one's seven!

OLD MAN. Four, five—

ANDY. This one's six!

OLD MAN. Slow down! One, two, three—

ANDY. Six!

OLD MAN. Four, five—

ANDY. Two twenty-five.

OLD MAN. One, two—

ANDY. Eight.

OLD MAN. You're confusin' me! One, two, three—

ANDY. Oh, what's the use? They're past due!

OLD MAN. All of them? But how can that be? I always pay my bills on time. I send you into town to…you ain't been payin' them?

ANDY. No.

OLD MAN. Why not?

ANDY. Because I hate doin' it. People are always laughin' and whisperin' behind my back! So from now on you do it. I quit! *(He crumples up the bill and throws it on the ground.)*

OLD MAN. Pick 'it up!

ANDY. No, you pick it up!

SALT. Andy?

OLD MAN. You march yourself to town and pay them bills right now!

ANDY. No! I told you I quit!

OLD MAN. You wanna go?

ANDY. Why is everythin' I do not good enough for you?

OLD MAN. Don't you talk to me that way! You ain't any better than me!

ANDY. You make everythin' so difficult!

OLD MAN. Garbage is garbage. That's where we come from but you wanna pretend you somethin' better?!

ANDY. What's wrong with that?

OLD MAN. You forget who you are!

ANDY. How can I when you remind me of it every day? "You just an Okie. Never amount to much."

SALT (picking up the delivery form). I can fix this letter!

ANDY. You always sayin', "You ain't got a lick of horse sense! You ain't good for nothin'!"

OLD MAN. I done it to make you strong!

ANDY. How? By tellin' me I'm no good?

SALT. I'll make it all better!

OLD MAN. People walk all over you if you let them.

ANDY. What are you so afraid of?

SALT. No more wrinkles!

OLD MAN. I ain't afraid of nothin'! You hear me? I kept you both here with me when your ma left!

ANDY. She was gonna take us with her but you wouldn't let her.

OLD MAN. I did it to protect you!

ANDY. Protect us from what? From the big bad world? Or were you just protectin' yourself?!

OLD MAN. You ain't got no right to say that!

ANDY. You're just an ignorant old fool holdin' on to nothin'!

SALT. It's gonna be as good as new!

OLD MAN. Don't you say another word!

ANDY. Made up lies and secrets! I'm sick of it!

SALT. See?

ANDY. And I ain't comin' back!

OLD MAN. Just like your ma!

ANDY. One day he's gonna leave you too!

OLD MAN. Get off my place!

ANDY. What are you gonna do then?

SALT. Andy?

ANDY. 'Cause you won't have nobody!

SALT. Grandpa?

ANDY. Nobody! *(Exits.)*

OLD MAN. He thinks he's so smart! That I'm stupid! Ignorant!

SALT. No, you're not, Grandpa.

OLD MAN. Spit on everythin' I done.

SALT. I don't like spittin'.

OLD MAN. He don't care nothin' 'bout us.

SALT. I do.

OLD MAN *(yelling)*. Don't you be here when I get back!

SALT. I'll help you, Grandpa. You can trust me.

OLD MAN. It's just I can't find my glasses.

SALT *(reading with difficulty)*. It says you gotta take twenty crates of lettuce to Hadley's. Ten crates of carrots to Friendly—

OLD MAN. —Corners.

SALT. Six crates to…

(They exit.)

SCENE 5

A car is heard passing by. HANNAH enters sticking out her thumb to catch a ride, but the car just passes her by. She climbs onto one of the letters and sits playing her guitar. ANDY rushes in with a pile of clothes and comic books. He drops them onto the floor.

HANNAH *(singing)*.
> **I built my lady a fine brick house**
> **I built it in a garden**
> **I put her in but she jumped out**
> **So fare ye well my darlin'**
>
> **Oh, swing a lady,**
> **Ump-tum**
> **Swing a lady,**
> **Round**
> **Swing a lady,**
> **Ump-tum**
> **And promenade around**

(SALT enters.)

SALT. Andy, Grandpa didn't mean none of those things!

ANDY. Of course he did.

SALT. He just a little mad 'cause he's got so much work to do. I can help from now on.

ANDY. It's all right, Salt.

SALT. I'll even wash them plates! You'll never have to ask me again!

ANDY. It's too late for that now.

SALT. Andy, please don't go!

(HANNAH begins writing a postcard.)

ANDY. I want you to have my favorite comic books.

SALT. No, I don't want 'em. I want you!

ANDY. I can't stay here no more. I gotta go.

SALT. No, please?!

ANDY. Look, Salt, you gonna have to grow up.

SALT. I will!

ANDY. You can't behave like a kid no more. I ain't gonna be around. All the old man ever does is put me down. Don't you let him tell you you're nothin', 'cause you're not.

SALT. But he loves us.

ANDY. He's got a funny way of showin' it. It's like he's built walls around himself. And they just keep gettin' higher and higher.

SALT. What walls?

ANDY. You gonna have to ask him yourself.

SALT. Ask him what?

ANDY. About his big fat secret.

SALT. Was I left on the porch step?

ANDY. What?

SALT. You said Grandpa found me on the porch step. Is that the big fat secret?

ANDY. Ain't you been listenin'?

SALT. Ugghhh! *(He pushes ANDY as hard as he can.)*

ANDY. What are you doin'?

SALT. You don't care nothin' about us!

ANDY. I care a lot.

SALT. Then why are you sayin' mean things?!

ANDY. 'Cause they're true!

SALT. No they're not! All you wanna to do is leave us! So go!

ANDY. If I don't I'll end up just like him. A broken-down old man just like his stupid truck. My future's out there and I ain't afraid to go after it.

SALT. What about me?

ANDY. You gonna be okay.

SALT. Why don't you take me with you?

ANDY. I can't.

SALT. That's 'cause you're selfish!

ANDY. I gotta do this alone, Salt.

SALT. You ain't my brother! "Family don't leave," that's what Grandpa says! I ain't ever leavin' him!

(SALT sits on the ground and covers his face. ANDY stops packing and brings over his comic books to SALT.)

SALT *(crying)*. I don't want your stupid stuff!

(SALT pushes him away. ANDY thinks for a moment. He removes a postcard from his pocket. HANNAH begins playing her guitar.)

HANNAH *(singing)*.
   Go to sleepy baby, Bye
   Go to sleepy baby, Bye

ANDY. Salt, what do you remember 'bout Ma?

HANNAH *(singing)*.
   Mama's goin' to the mailboat

SALT. Lots of things.

HANNAH *(singing)*.
> **Mama's goin' to the mailboat, Bye**

ANDY. How could you? You were just a baby.

HANNAH *(singing)*.
> **Bye ole baby, Bye**

SALT. So?

HANNAH *(singing)*.
> **Bye ole baby, Bye**

ANDY. She liked to sing.
SALT. No she didn't.

HANNAH *(singing)*.
> **Papa's goin' to the mailboat**
> **Papa's goin' to the mailboat, bye**

ANDY. How would you know? All you did was eat, sleep and poop.
SALT. Be quiet.
ANDY. She'd hold you in her arms and rock you to sleep every night. Her hair was long and messy. She liked suckin' on red popsicles and givin' us butterfly kisses. She could skip rocks on the water, climb trees and make funny animal noises.
SALT. What kind?
ANDY. She could do a duck.

(ANDY and HANNAH imitate a duck sound.)

ANDY. A dog.

(ANDY and HANNAH imitate a dog barking.)

ANDY. And a cow.

(ANDY and HANNAH imitate a cow.)

ANDY. But most of all she loved singing and playin' on her guitar.

(HANNAH sticks her thumb out hoping to hitch a ride. The car just passes by. HANNAH plays softly.)

SALT. I remember sunlight.
ANDY. Sunlight?
SALT. She made me feel safe and sleepy.
ANDY. That's 'cause we all slept in the same bed.
SALT. Grandpa says she sang at the Grand Ole Opry.
ANDY. I got a postcard from there. You wanna see it?
SALT. Okay.
HANNAH. Dear Daddy, this here is where I'm gonna make my professional debut.
ANDY. The old man used to tell us all the places she'd been to by the postcards she sent us.
HANNAH. I get nervous just thinkin' about it.

(The OLD MAN enters holding a postcard. He is a memory.)

OLD MAN. Your ma sent you boys another postcard. Now, hold on. I reckon she must be playin' her music there. Yup, that's what it must be. You can see it's a rich people's place. How? Well, that's easy. Look at them lawns. They're nice and straight. And they got fancy flowers growin' all over.

SALT. Andy, how did Ma die?

ANDY. In a car accident. A state trooper told the old man and me she was headin' back home to us.

OLD MAN. Them rich people places ain't no place for us, but your mama knows how to talk real nice. I bet you she's got a dress for every day of the year and suitcases bigger than this house! And one day, she's gonna come ridin' back here in a big ol' bus with her name written all over it.

HANNAH. "Hannah Holcomb"!

(The OLD MAN exits.)

HANNAH. I've been workin' at all sort of jobs.

ANDY. I want you to keep this for me.

HANNAH. I'll send money as soon as I can.

ANDY. This is all I got of her, I don't know what ever happened to them other postcards. So you gotta take care of it.

SALT. Okay.

HANNAH. Tell my babies I love them.

ANDY. Salt? I gotta go now.

SALT *(crying)*. Who's gonna make me colored pancakes?

ANDY. You're gonna have to learn yourself. And one day you'll leave too. Just like me and Ma.

SALT. No. He needs me.

ANDY. I don't wanna end up like him. Can you under-
    stand that?
SALT. No.
ANDY. I'm goin'.
SALT *(grabs ANDY's leg tightly)*. No...
ANDY. Let go!
SALT. No!

*(ANDY tears SALT away from him. He grabs his grocery
bag of clothes and exits.)*

ANDY. I'll write you!
SALT. Andy, don't go!

HANNAH *(singing)*.
    Bye ole baby, Bye
    Bye ole baby, Bye
    Papa's goin' to the mailboat
    Papa's goin' to the mailboat, Bye

SALT. Andy! *(SALT stands there alone holding the post-
    card.)*

SCENE 6

*Blue sky and white clouds. It's a beautiful day. PEP-
PER, a young Latina girl dressed like a boy, appears.
She wears a hat. She carries a stack of books. She
chooses her place. She picks her most favorite book, and
kicks her shoes off. She lies on one of the large letters,
wiggles her toes, and starts to read. SALT enters carry-*

ing a fishing pole. He's in a foul mood. He stops in shock seeing the two feet. He picks up a shoe and throws it back.

PEPPER *(sitting up)*. Ow!

SALT. This is my spot!

PEPPER. …

SALT. My spot!

PEPPER. …

SALT. Hello, you talk English?!

PEPPER. …

SALT. Go! Get outta of here! Vamoose!

PEPPER. You vamoose! I don't see a sign anywhere with your name on it.

SALT. I don't need a sign! This is my secret spot!

PEPPER. Says "who"?

SALT. Says me!

PEPPER. I'm not leavin'.

SALT. I ain't warnin' you again!

PEPPER. I was here first! *(SALT grabs PEPPER's book.)* Give me back my book!

SALT. Not until you go!

PEPPER. I was here first!

SALT. "To my best pupil, Pepper…"

PEPPER. That's private!

SALT. "Best wishes, Mrs. Federico."

PEPPER. Give it back to me!

SALT. What kinda stupid name is that?

PEPPER. You're asking for it!

SALT. No, you are!

(SALT throws PEPPER's book offstage into the creek.)

PEPPER. Agghhh!

*(PEPPER charges SALT. They start wrestling. In the me-
lee PEPPER's hat is torn off and her hair falls onto her
shoulders. SALT stops.)*

SALT. You're a girl!
PEPPER. That's right, you moron!

(PEPPER decks SALT. He falls to the ground.)

SALT. Ow!
PEPPER *(upset)*. Why did you throw my book into the creek?
SALT. You wouldn't leave.
PEPPER. It's gone!
SALT. Serves you right. I warned you.
PEPPER *(crying)*. That was my most favorite book.
SALT. Stop whinin'. It's just a stupid book.

(PEPPER decks SALT again.)

SALT. Ow!
PEPPER. It's not a "stupid" book. It's one of a kind. It
    can't be replaced!
SALT. So what?
PEPPER. My teacher gave it to me as a going away pres-
    ent. And now it's lost forever! You are so mean.
SALT. I told you this was my spot!
PEPPER. How was I supposed to know?
SALT. What are you, a pecan picker?
PEPPER. I am not a pecan picker!
SALT. Bet your dad is.

PEPPER. No, he isn't!

SALT. Bet you live in those old barracks on Castro Hill?

PEPPER. No, we don't!

SALT. Bet your dad don't even speak English!

PEPPER. I hate this place and I hate you!

SALT. I hate you too, Pecan Picker!

(PEPPER picks up her stack of books and exits crying.)

SALT. Dumb girl! Stupid book! My spot!

SCENE 7

HANNAH enters. She wears a waitress dress and pours a cup of coffee to an imaginary customer. Simultaneously the OLD MAN enters carrying several wooden crates of produce. He stops to wipe his forehead. He no longer wears his arm sling.

HANNAH *(singing)*.
> **Johnny get your hair cut**
> **hair cut, hair cut**
> **Johnny get your hair cut**
> **Just like me**
>
> **Johnny get your hair cut**
> **hair cut, hair cut**
> **Johnny get your hair cut**
> **Just like me**

(ANDY enters marching, wearing Marine fatigues. HAN-NAH takes an order. The OLD MAN removes a delivery form from his pocket and tries to make sense of it, but can't. In frustration he crumples it, throwing it away.)

HANNAH *(singing).*
> **Johnny get your gun**
> **And your sword**
> **And your pistol**
>
> **Johnny get your gun**
> **And come with me**
>
> **Johnny get your gun**
> **And your sword**
> **And your pistol**
>
> **Johnny get your gun**
> **And come with me**

(HANNAH pours another cup of coffee while ANDY continues marching. SALT runs in to help the OLD MAN carry away the crates.)

HANNAH & ANDY *(singing).*
> **Hey, ya Betty Martin tiptoe, tiptoe**
> **Hey, ya Betty Martin tiptoe, tiptoe-fy**
> **Hey, ya Betty Martin tiptoe, tiptoe-fy**
>
> **Hey, ya Betty Martin tiptoe, tiptoe**
> **Hey, ya Betty Martin tiptoe, tiptoe-fy**
> **Hey, ya Betty Martin tiptoe, tiptoe-fy**

(SALT, the OLD MAN and HANNAH exit. ANDY sits on his helmet and begins writing a postcard. SALT enters looking at a postcard. He climbs onto one of the letters to read.)

ANDY. February 17th, 1952. Dear Salt—I told you I'd write.

SALT. "This is a postcard from San Die…go."

ANDY. It's a pretty place with lots of blue ocean and sandy beaches.

SALT. "You must be won…der…in' what I'm doin' out here."

ANDY. Well, surprise, I joined the U.S. Marine Corps!

SALT. Why'd you do that?

ANDY. To show the old man he's wrong. They did take me. Besides I like it. The food's great. The sarge reminds me of the old man 'cause he's always yellin' at me. Grandpa woulda made a good Marine.

SALT. Of course he would.

ANDY. I never thought I'd miss him and home so much. Can you believe that?

SALT. No.

ANDY. I'll be in boot camp for a few more months, and then I'll get stationed somewhere I hope is—

SALT. "Ex…o…tic"?

ANDY. Somewhere there's sandy beaches and plenty of—

SALT / ANDY *(together)*. —girls? / —girls!

SALT. Ughh…

ANDY. Yup! You made any friends yet?

SALT. No.

ANDY. You ain't still mad at me, are you?

SALT. …

ANDY. Will you write me?

(SALT tears up the postcard. He begins to leave but returns picking it up.)

SCENE 8

PEPPER enters taking off her shoes. She rolls up her pants legs. She searches for her book. SALT enters carrying a fishing pole.

SALT. Not you again!

PEPPER. I ain't standin' near your stupid "spot"!

SALT. I can see that.

PEPPER. Did you come to laugh at me?

SALT. No. What you lookin' for?

PEPPER. I'm looking for my book! You remember my book, don't you? My most favorite one!

(SALT pulls out PEPPER's book and looks at it.)

SALT. Yes, I do. Them rocks are slippery. You better be careful.

PEPPER. It's gotta be here somewhere.

SALT. You ain't gonna find it.

PEPPER. Yes, I will!

SALT. It mighta floated all the way out to sea.

PEPPER. Go away.

SALT. Maybe all them words slipped off them book pages and now they're fish food.

PEPPER. That ain't funny.

SALT. Or maybe some hobo's used your book to make himself a warm toasty fire.

PEPPER *(sarcastically).* Huh, huh! *(She falls into the creek.)*
   Aaghhh!

SALT. Told you them rocks were slippery.

PEPPER. Oh, darn it! I give up!

SALT. Here. *(Hands PEPPER her book.)*

PEPPER. You found my book?

SALT. I didn't throw it that far.

PEPPER. It's dry.

SALT. My brother Andy and me once had all our comic
   books get rained on and we hung them up on a clothes-
   line and they were almost good as new.

PEPPER. Almost as good?

SALT. Your book was too heavy so I put it near the stove
   and it dried real fast. 'Cept the outside got a little crispy.

PEPPER. Oh, no.

SALT. But the pages aren't stickin' together. I'm sorry I
   threw your book into the creek.

PEPPER. Why are you bein' nice? Did you get into trouble
   or somethin'?

SALT. No.

PEPPER. This ain't a stupid boy trick, is it?

SALT. No.

PEPPER. 'Cause if you're tryin' to make fun of me—

SALT. I ain't.

PEPPER. I'll hit you even harder.

SALT. I'm really sorry. Honest.

PEPPER. You go to church or somethin'?

SALT. No.

PEPPER. I don't understand why you're bein' so friendly?

SALT. There's nobody else to play with around here.

PEPPER. I noticed.

SALT. All everybody does is work. Work before the sun comes up. Work 'til the sun goes down. They might as well work while they sleep too.

PEPPER. My daddy's got me cookin' meals everyday. Cook and wash. Cook and wash. Sometimes I wish someone would make me somethin'.

SALT. Like what?

PEPPER. Somethin' fancy. Somethin' sweet!

SALT. Like pancakes?

PEPPER. Yeah, pancakes!

SALT. I can show you how.

PEPPER. Okay.

SALT. I'm sorry I called your daddy a pecan picker.

PEPPER. You wanna know somethin'?

SALT. What?

PEPPER. My daddy is a pecan picker. And a lettuce picker. And an apple picker.

SALT. All three?

PEPPER. Sometimes a strawberry picker too.

SALT. I like strawberries.

PEPPER. I don't. They turn your fingers all red and sticky and you can only eat so many before you feel sick.

SALT. My grandpa used to pick pecans but now he drives a produce truck. I get to go with him lots of places. Where'd you learn to fight?

PEPPER. I have four big brothers. I'm the only girl.

SALT. You hit like a boy.

PEPPER. My father taught me how to box. You wanna learn?

SALT. No, thanks.

PEPPER. My name's Pepper.

SALT. Mine's Salt.

(They burst out laughing.)

SALT. That's funny!

PEPPER. We're named after spices!

SALT. Pepper ought to be a boy's name.

PEPPER *(holding up her fist at SALT)*. You got a problem with it?

SALT. Not no more.

PEPPER. Good. So how'd you get stuck with the name Salt?

SALT. I like eatin' it on everythin'. Lots of it. What about you?

PEPPER. I'm named after my grandma on my father's side. Her name was Josefina, but they called her *Pepita*.

SALT. That's a funny sorta name.

PEPPER. That's why I changed it to Pepper. 'Cause pepper has got a kick to it.

SALT. So what do you like to do?

PEPPER. I like to climb trees. Swap for things. Skip rocks on water, and watch clouds pass by. But most of all I like readin' books.

SALT. I hate reading.

PEPPER. When I was little, I use to love chewin' on paper. My daddy says I chewed so much that I got all them letters and words floatin' in my head now. That's why I like piecin' them together. Easy as pie.

SALT. Well, it ain't so easy for me. Every time I try puttin' them letters together they just seem to float away. Nothin' makes sense. I feel stupid and the kids at school know it. That's why I hate school.

PEPPER. I don't. I'd miss it.

SALT. Why?

PEPPER. 'Cause I miss my teachers and friends. Just when I feel happy in one place, my daddy picks up and goes.

SALT. Goes where?

PEPPER. Anywhere there's a crop to pick. I hate movin'. That's why I pretend I'm in school 'cause I can visit my friends and teachers and feel normal. One day, when I grow up, I wanna be a school librarian 'cause they sit and read all day and sip tea like the English.

SALT. I wanna be just like my grandpa. He's pretty smart. Can fix anythin'.

PEPPER. My daddy too.

SALT. So what's your book about?

PEPPER. It's about a princess, a shoemaker's apprentice, a castle and a green-colored dragon. I even got me a collection of books. I got happy books. Sad books. Adventure books. And even fairy tale books.

SALT. I like comic books better.

PEPPER. I like 'em too. Maybe we could swap some time. *(She opens her book. Torn pieces of a postcard fall out.)* What's this?

SALT. Oh, that's mine.

PEPPER. What is it?

SALT. It's a postcard.

PEPPER. It's all in pieces.

(SALT pieces the postcard together.)

SALT. That's 'cause I tore it up.

PEPPER. Why'd you do that?

SALT. 'Cause I'm mad at my brother.

PEPPER. Does he know you're mad at him?

SALT. I don't know.

PEPPER. You should write to him.

SALT. What for?

PEPPER. So you can tell him how you feel. Besides, when somebody writes to you, you're supposed to write back. It's polite.

SALT. I don't know what to say. Besides I can't write too good.

PEPPER. All you need is an address, some paper, an envelope and a little bitty stamp. I can show you, if you want?

SALT. I don't know.

PEPPER. I like the picture of the palm trees and sandy beach. Can I keep it?

SALT. No.

PEPPER. But you tore it up.

SALT. I'm gonna glue it back together.

PEPPER. I'll swap you for it.

SALT. Nah. *(He puts the postcard pieces in his pocket.)* Pepper, you like fishin'?

PEPPER. Ah huh.

SALT. You wanna fish?

PEPPER. Okay.

SALT. Do you like catchin' fish?

PEPPER. Nope.

SALT. Do you like cookin' fish?

PEPPER. Nope.

SALT. Well, what do you like about fishin' then?

PEPPER. Eatin' 'em!

SCENE 9

HANNAH enters. She throws small paper letters into the air.

HANNAH *(singing).*
Hush 'n' Bye
Don't you cry
Oh, you pretty little babies

OLD MAN *(offstage).* Hannah?

HANNAH *(singing).*
When you wake
You'll get sweet cake
And all the pretty little ponies

OLD MAN *(offstage).* Hannah?

HANNAH *(singing).*
A brown and a grey
And a black and a bay
All the pretty little ponies

(The OLD MAN appears. He is half dressed in overalls and carries a lantern.)

HANNAH. Ain't it beautiful, Daddy?
OLD MAN. Honey, it's the middle of the night.
HANNAH. And it's rainin' letters again.
OLD MAN. Letters?
HANNAH. In all shapes and sizes mixed together.

OLD MAN. You gonna catch yourself a cold.

(ANDY appears. He is also a memory. Dressed in his civilian clothes, he carries a crate of envelopes.)

ANDY. I've packed these for you, see?
OLD MAN. Andy, what are you doin'?
ANDY. Truckloads full of 'em.
HANNAH. Ain't it the most beautiful thing you ever seen?
OLD MAN. Let me see your forehead.
HANNAH & ANDY. I ain't got a fever!

(HANNAH rushes away from him throwing letters into the air. ANDY throws the envelopes onto the ground.)

OLD MAN. Why are you here?
ANDY. I'm unloadin' crates of made-up lies and secrets.
HANNAH. Daddy, there isn't much time.
ANDY. You got so many.
OLD MAN. Take 'em back.
HANNAH. You ain't makin' sense, Daddy.
ANDY. They're gonna bury you alive.
OLD MAN. Andy, I need your help.
ANDY. You ain't good for nothin'.
ANDY & HANNAH. Garbage is garbage. Don't you remember?
OLD MAN. I was wrong.
HANNAH. It's a dream, Daddy.
ANDY. Ignorant old fool!
HANNAH. Ignorant old fool!
OLD MAN. Andy, please don't go!
HANNAH. It's in the postcards, Daddy.

OLD MAN. Hannah, bring him back!

HANNAH. All you gotta do is read them.

(ANDY and HANNAH laugh at him. They exit.)

OLD MAN. Hannah! Andy!

(SALT enters.)

SALT. Grandpa?

OLD MAN. Did you see your brother?

SALT. Andy?

OLD MAN. He was just here, and so was your ma.

SALT. Ma? Grandpa, you got a fever?

OLD MAN. They was just here. Go find 'em.

SALT. What are all these bills doin' on the floor?

OLD MAN. Never mind.

SALT. Why haven't you opened them?

OLD MAN. I ain't had time.

SALT. This one's from the bank. And this one's from the feed store.

OLD MAN. Them little bitty letters are hard to read. You know, I can never find my glasses!

SALT. I found 'em. I found 'em yesterday under the truck seat. Here. *(He gives the OLD MAN his glasses. SALT tears open an envelope.)*

OLD MAN. I wonder how they got there?

SALT. Ain't you gonna read it?

OLD MAN. This one is from the…the…

SALT *(unsure)*. Feed store?

OLD MAN. That's right. And they want me to pay my bill.

SALT. How much is it?

OLD MAN. I owe 'em three dollars and twenty-five cents.

SALT. That doesn't sound like the feed store.

OLD MAN. No?

SALT. Let me see, Grandpa. It's from the bank and it ain't three dollars and twenty-five cents.

OLD MAN. It's not?

SALT. It's three hundred and twenty-five dollars! It says you're "past due."

OLD MAN. What? That ain't my fault! Andy should be here! He sorts the bills. I count the money! That's the way it's always been.

SALT. Grandpa, what's goin' on?

OLD MAN. Nothin'. Everythin's all right. Go to sleep.

SALT. What does this one say?

OLD MAN. It ain't your business! Now, go to bed!

SALT. You can't read, can you?!

OLD MAN. No, that ain't true!

SALT. Yes, it is! You can't read and they're gonna take everythin' away from us!

OLD MAN. That's not how it is!

SALT. Grandpa, why didn't you tell me?

OLD MAN. You gotta help me sort this out, Salt.

SALT. Andy knew all along, didn't he? That's your big fat secret.

OLD MAN. You tell me what them bills say and I'll count the—

SALT. Andy loved you and so did Ma. But you drove them away!

OLD MAN. No.

SALT. You lied to me. I hate you, Grandpa!

OLD MAN. You don't mean that!

SALT. Andy was right about you. You're just an ignorant old fool!

OLD MAN. Salt!

(SALT exits.)

OLD MAN. Salt, you don't know what it's like goin' around not knowin' what things say! Scared of what people think. Makin' excuses all the time. Pretendin' you know what things mean but don't. Salt? *(Exits.)*

SCENE 10

Blue sky and white clouds. SALT and PEPPER enter. They carry a fishing pole and are walking barefoot.

SALT. Pepper, it ain't workin'!

PEPPER. You gotta wiggle your nose more.

SALT. I don't feel any better.

PEPPER. You just gotta give it time. Try wigglin' your ears.

SALT. No.

PEPPER. Well, it always works for me. Try wigglin' your toes.

SALT. I don't wanna.

PEPPER. You gotta let the air circulate around them.

SALT. Why?

PEPPER. To cool off. That way you'll feel better. I do this whenever I get upset.

SALT. I thought my grandpa was the smartest man in the whole world.

PEPPER. You can't be mad at him forever, you know?

SALT. Why not?

PEPPER. 'Cause you live in the same house.

SALT. He's a big fat liar. Pretendin' he knows everythin' but he don't know nothin'. He can't even read a road sign. That's why he wrecked his truck.

PEPPER. It don't mean he's stupid. Maybe he never learned how to read. My daddy never did, but he knows now.

SALT. How'd he do that?

PEPPER. I taught him one letter at a time.

SALT. One letter at a time?

PEPPER. Ah huh. Then that letter turned into a word, then that word turned into a sentence, which added up to a paragraph, which turned into a page, and then a whole book. Here, I got somethin' for you. *(She hands SALT a small wrapped package.)*

SALT. What is it?

PEPPER. Just say "thank you" and open it.

SALT. Thank you. *(He opens it, finding paper, a pencil, some envelopes. And some stamps.)*

PEPPER. It's so you can write to Andy and anybody else that you want to.

SALT. Who else would I want to write to?

PEPPER. Me.

SALT. You?

PEPPER. My daddy's fixin' to leave soon.

SALT. You too?

PEPPER. Pecan season is almost finished. I thought, if I showed you how to write a letter, maybe you want to write back.

SALT. We ain't boyfriend and girlfriend, are we?

PEPPER. No!

SALT. 'Cause I hate girls.

PEPPER. And I hate boys.

SALT. We just friends.

PEPPER. Friends.

SALT. Okay, I'll write you. But you gotta show me how.

PEPPER. Let's start by writin' to Andy.

SALT. I don't know what to say to him.

PEPPER. Tell him how you feel.

SALT. All I got to say is awful things about my grandpa.

PEPPER. That's a start.

SALT. What is?

PEPPER. "Dear Andy, Grandpa is an idiot! Love, Salt."

SALT. Are you makin' fun of me?!

PEPPER. No. It helps to write out what you feel.

SALT. I can't spell too good.

PEPPER. It don't matter. I'll help.

SALT. I don't know how to start.

PEPPER. Start with "Dear Andy."

SALT. That's stupid!

PEPPER. Then you do it!

(Pause.)

SALT. I'm sorry.

PEPPER. I'll write. You just talk.

SALT. "Dear Andy…"

PEPPER. "Dear Andy…"

SALT. "How are you?"

PEPPER. "How are you?" Now tell him how you feel.

SALT. "I am fine."

PEPPER. Now, tell him…

SALT. Who's writin' this letter?

PEPPER. You are.

SALT. Then let me say what I gotta say!

PEPPER. Okay!

SALT. "I wish I could see you. Nothin' has been the same since you left."

PEPPER *(overlapping)*. "Nothin' has been the same."

SALT. "Why didn't you…"

PEPPER. "…didn't you…"

SALT. "…tell me…"

PEPPER. "….tell me…" Slow down!

SALT. "…about Grandpa?"

PEPPER. "…about Grandpa?"

SALT. "Your brother, Salt."

PEPPER. That's it?

SALT. Yup.

PEPPER. Don't you want ask him what he's doin'? Where he's been?

SALT. Nope.

PEPPER. You got a lot more room still left, you know?

SALT. That's all I wanna say. It's my letter, right?

PEPPER. Right. Don't you wanna draw a picture of somethin'?

SALT. Pepper!

PEPPER. Okay!

SALT *(leans back and wiggles his toes)*. My toes feel better.

(HANNAH appears playing her guitar. A moment later, ANDY enters carrying his duffel bag. He reads a post-card.)

SALT. I got another postcard from Andy.

ANDY. May 6th, 1952. Dear Salt—

(The OLD MAN enters carrying a small shoebox. He opens it. It is filled with dozens of postcards.)

HANNAH. Daddy, where do I begin? How do I explain my life to you? The choices I've made?

ANDY. I should've told you about the old man, but I couldn't. You're always lookin' up to him. I'm sorry I didn't.

HANNAH. My life has been a sorry state of affairs. And I know how it's saddened you.

ANDY. He carries a big hurt inside. It's shaped the way he is and the way he's treated us.

HANNAH. I'm sorry for causin' you so much heartache. And I'm sorry for the mean things I said.

ANDY. I wish I could help him, but I've never known what to do.

HANNAH. I'm so thankful that my boys are with you. I was pretty mad at you for the longest time.

ANDY. But don't be too angry at him.

HANNAH. God, how I miss their smiles and their little warm bodies sleepin' next to me.

ANDY. He loves you, you know?

HANNAH. I think Andy took my leavin' the hardest. I know he cried when I left. I could feel him in my heart.

ANDY. I'm shippin' out soon. Thought I was gonna see sandy beaches and girls. Just my luck. I'm goin' to Korea.

HANNAH. A child shouldn't have to grow up so quickly in this world.

ANDY. You ever heard of Korea?

SALT. No.

PEPPER. Me either.

HANNAH. Daddy, I hope you can get somebody to read this for you. And if you're not too mad at me, would you mind lettin' me come back home?

ANDY. Your brother—

HANNAH. Your little girl—

ANDY / HANNAH *(together)*. —Andy. / —Hannah.

(HANNAH and ANDY exit. The OLD MAN continues to look at the postcards.)

PEPPER. You miss him, don't you?

SALT. A whole lot. I keep thinkin' if maybe I could of done somethin' more Andy would still he here. Things would be just the way they used to be.

PEPPER. Salt, it ain't your fault Andy left.

SALT. Why didn't I wash them dishes!

PEPPER. You really think it would've mattered?

SALT. Maybe. I don't know. No.

PEPPER. It was just his time to go, Salt. I bet your grandpa misses him too.

SALT. Why would he?

PEPPER. Maybe he thinks it's his fault Andy left 'cause, you know—

SALT. You really think so?

PEPPER. Maybe if you showed him how, you could write to Andy together.

SALT. I can hardly read and write myself. How am I gonna teach him?

PEPPER. One letter at a time. Remember? All you gotta do is ask.

SALT. Okay.

(They begin to exit.)

SALT. Pepper?

PEPPER. Yeah?

SALT. Thanks for the present.

(They run off. HANNAH's voice is heard singing. The OLD MAN enters with a shoebox. He looks at the postcards. SALT enters. The OLD MAN hides the shoebox. SALT holds out the postcard he had torn up earlier. It has been glued back together.)

SALT. Andy sent this.

OLD MAN. Andy?

SALT. He wrote to me.

OLD MAN. It's all tore up.

SALT. That's 'cause I did it.

OLD MAN. You still mad at him?

SALT. Not no more. Are you?

(Beat.)

OLD MAN. What's it say?

SALT. He joined the Marine Corps.

OLD MAN. He did?

SALT. He misses us. I've been thinkin', maybe if we write to him he'll wanna come back home and live with us again, you think?

OLD MAN. That's up to him, Salt.

SALT. If he wanted to, would it be all right with you?

OLD MAN. Family is family.

SALT. You really mean that?

OLD MAN. Yup.

SALT. Grandpa, who taught Andy to make colored pancakes? Was it Ma?

OLD MAN. No.

SALT. Was it you?

OLD MAN. …

SALT. You gonna teach me?

OLD MAN. Maybe.

SALT. You wanna help me write Andy a letter?

OLD MAN. I got lots of things to do.

SALT. It won't take long. I know how.

OLD MAN. I got all them bills to pay and produce to deliver.

SALT. I'll help you after we write Andy.

OLD MAN. I'm behind already. The day's begun and—

SALT. Okay.

OLD MAN. Go on now. Get yourself to school.

(SALT begins to exit.)

OLD MAN. Salt?

SALT. Yeah, Grandpa?

OLD MAN. You study hard. Learn them books.

(SALT exits.)

SCENE 11

SALT enters flipping the blue pancake high into the air.

SALT. Hurry up, Pepper. The pancake's ready!

(PEPPER enters carrying a plate filled with colored pancakes. They both wear pots on their heads.)

PEPPER. It's my turn to flip!
SALT. Okay, I'll catch!

(They switch. PEPPER flips the blue pancake high into the air…)

SALT. Wo!
PEPPER. Wo!

(…as SALT catches it on the plate. PEPPER pounds a beat on her frying pan as SALT and PEPPER do a victory dance.)

PEPPER. Salt, how many postcards you got from Andy now?
SALT. Ten.
PEPPER. You wanna swap for 'em? I got thirty Lincoln pennies I found on Stevens Road. My daddy says it'll bring a whole lot of luck. You can make wishes and they'll come true.
SALT. How do you know that?
PEPPER. 'Cause I made thirty of 'em and they all came true.
SALT. No they didn't!

PEPPER. Yes, they did!

SALT. What'd you wish for?

PEPPER. I can't tell you that. Wishes are supposed to be secrets. They don't come true if you tell. Everythin' gets undone. So you wanna trade or not?

SALT. Okay, but just for a little while.

(They swap.)

PEPPER. Good trade.

SALT. Even trade.

PEPPER. Now, make a wish.

(SALT makes a wish.)

PEPPER. I know what your wish is!

SALT. I'm not sayin'.

PEPPER. You wished for—

SALT. Air raid!

PEPPER. Oh, no!

SALT & PEPPER *(duck for cover)*. Pa-pow! Pa-pow! Pa-pow! Pa-pa-pa-pa-pow!

SALT. We ain't gonna make it, Pepper!

PEPPER. This is our last stand!

SALT & PEPPER. Pa-pow! Pa-pow! Pa-pow! Pa-pa-pa-pa-pow!

(ANDY enters wearing battle fatigues, backpack and helmet.)

ANDY. Dear Salt. Last night I was eatin' my dinner out of a can, and it was good!

SALT & PEPPER. Pa-pow! Pa-pow! Pa-pow! Pa-pa-pa-pa-pow!

ANDY. But I wish I had some salt and pepper. Like you and your friend.

SALT. Ughhh!!! I'm hit!

PEPPER. Me too!

ANDY. Salt and Pepper. You can't have one without the other.

(An explosion lands nearby. ANDY exits. SALT dies a horrible death scene. PEPPER does an even more horrible and dramatic death scene. She knocks something over and the OLD MAN's shoebox is revealed.)

PEPPER. What's this?

SALT. It's a shoebox.

PEPPER. What's inside?

SALT *(picks it up and shakes it)*. It don't sound like shoes.

PEPPER. Do you think we should open it?

SALT. Could be dangerous.

PEPPER. Real dangerous, huh?

SALT & PEPPER. Let's open it! *(They open the box.)*

SALT. They're postcards.

PEPPER. There's a whole lot of them. Who's "Daddy"?

SALT. Let me see.

PEPPER. Who they from?

SALT. From my ma.

PEPPER. Your ma?

(They look at the postcards as HANNAH enters. She holds a mop. She looks around cautiously.)

HANNAH. Hello, is anybody here?

SALT. This one's from the Grand Ole Opry.

HANNAH. Hello?

PEPPER. Where's that?

SALT. Nashville.

(HANNAH curtsies to an imaginary audience. She holds the mop as if it's a microphone.)

HANNAH. It's a great honor to be here with you tonight. I wanna say hello to my little ones back home and to my daddy. I made it! I wanna sing this little song I'm dedicatin' to them. *(She holds her mop like a guitar. Sings.)*

Oh, sister Phoebe
How merry were we
The night we sat
Under the Juniper Tree
The Juniper Tree
Hi-ho, hi-ho
The Juniper Tree
Hi-ho...

(The OLD MAN enters.)

OLD MAN. Salt, what are you doin' with that?

SALT. We found it.

PEPPER. It was an accident, Mr. Holcomb.

OLD MAN. That belongs to me.

SALT. These postcards are from my ma, aren't they?

OLD MAN. Yup.

SALT. Why are you hidin' them?

OLD MAN. 'Cause it's all I got left of your ma. I don't know what they say. You see, her life wasn't easy. She was just a girl when she had Andy. Then you come along. I wasn't the most understandin' daddy. My little Hannah tried to set her life straight, but she never could. One day she just packed off and left. Maybe she tried to sing, maybe she didn't.

SALT. All them stories about my ma, are they lies?

OLD MAN. I made them up so you would he proud of her. So you wouldn't be ashamed. She was always singin' and laughin' with you boys. Your ma did have the prettiest voice you ever heard. I ain't lyin' about that.

SALT. So my ma was never a famous singer?

OLD MAN. No.

HANNAH. Hello, is anybody out there? *(She takes her mop and exits.)*

SALT. And she never sang at the Grand Ole Opry either?

OLD MAN. I'm not really sure. All I got left are these postcards from your ma. And I don't even know what they say. I'm sorry I lied to you and Andy. Once you tell a lie it only gets bigger and bigger until it buries you.

(SOUND: Another explosion is heard. Then "Taps" is heard played from an acoustic guitar. ANDY enters in a Marine uniform holding an American flag under his arm. He stands at attention.)

OLD MAN. I got this today. Looks important. Tell me what it says.

SALT. "Dear Mr. Holcomb, it is with my deepest regret I have to inform you that your grandson—"

ANDY. Corporal Andrew Holcomb was killed in action—

OLD MAN. Andy.

ANDY. In Korea, on December 12th, 1952.

SALT. "Your grandson was under my command. And I am proud to say I knew him well. He spoke highly of both you and his little brother." *(SALT hands the letter to PEPPER.)*

ANDY. He talked of going home, learning the family business, and cooking colored pancakes for his little brother and best friend.

PEPPER. "Andrew was a brave young man, and a proud Marine. Signed, Thomas R. Murrow, Captain, United States Marine Corps."

(ANDY places the folded American flag on the shoebox. He steps back and salutes. He exits. The OLD MAN sits quietly.)

PEPPER *(reaches for SALT's hand)*. I'm sorry, Salt.

SALT. I know.

PEPPER. You want to go to the creek or somethin'?

SALT. No.

PEPPER. Maybe, we could go fishin', huh?

SALT. No thanks.

(The OLD MAN removes the flag and opens the shoebox.)

OLD MAN. Times were hard when I was a boy. My daddy didn't believe schoolin' was important. So he took me to work. And that's all I've ever known. But he was wrong. I've been ashamed all my life because I couldn't read. And I've ruined everythin' I've ever loved because of it.

SALT. Not everythin', Grandpa.

OLD MAN. Will you teach me to read? *(He hands SALT a postcard. A guitar is heard playing softly.)*
SALT. Okay. But I'm gonna need Pepper's help.
OLD MAN. What do you say, Pepper?
PEPPER. It would he my honor.
OLD MAN. I wanna learn to read my little Hannah's post-cards. Can you teach me that?
SALT & PEPPER. One letter at a time.

(HANNAH appears.)

HANNAH *(singing)*.
    Hush 'n' Bye
    Don't you cry
    Oh, you pretty little babies

OLD MAN. Where do we start?
SALT. That's the letter "D."
OLD MAN. "D."

HANNAH *(singing.*
    When you wake
    You'll get sweet cake
    And all the pretty little ponies

PEPPER. That's the letter "a."
OLD MAN. …a…

HANNAH *(singing)*.
    A brown and a grey
    And a black and a bay
    All the pretty little ponies

SALT. …"d."
OLD MAN. …d…

(ANDY appears in his uniform.)

HANNAH & ANDY *(singing)*.
> **Hush 'n' Bye**
> **Don't you cry**
> **Oh, you pretty little babies**

OLD MAN. There's another "d."
PEPPER. Ah huh.

HANNAH & ANDY *(singing)*.
> **When you wake**
> **You'll have sweet cake**
> **And all the pretty little ponies**

SALT. …"y."
OLD MAN. …y…

HANNAH & ANDY *(singing)*.
> **And a black and a bay**
> **A brown and a grey**
> **All the pretty little ponies**

SALT. That word means "Daddy."
OLD MAN. Daddy. So that's what that little word looks
   like? Imagine that? *(The OLD MAN smiles.)*

END OF PLAY

Hush 'n' Bye

cue: start of the show, curtain opens

Moderate ♩= 60

Hannah   Hush 'n' bye,   don't you cry   Oh, you pret-ty lit-tle ba - by,

When you wake you'll have sweet cake, And all the pret-ty lit-tle pon - ies, A

brown and a gray and a black and a bay, And all the pret-ty lit-tle pon - ies

Built My Lady a Fine Brick House

cue: Andy rushes in with a pile of clothes and books and drops them to the floor

Moderately fast ♩= 104

Hannah   Built my la-dy a fine brick house, Built it in a gar-den, I put her in but

she jumped out, So fare ye well, my darl-ing Oh, swing a la-dy ump - tum,

swing a la-dy round, Swing a la-dy ump - tum and prom-e-nade a-round

Go to Sleep

cue: Salt - "I don't want your stupid stuff!"
Andy - Thinks for a moment and removes a card from his pocket

Johnny Get Your Hair Cut

cue: Old man enters carrying produce. He stops to wipe his forehead.

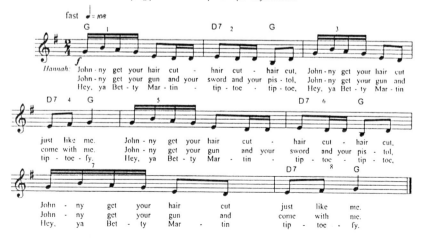

The Juniper Tree

cue: Hannah - "I made it! I wanna sing this little song I'm dedicatin" to them."

DIRECTOR'S NOTES

DIRECTOR'S NOTES

DIRECTOR'S NOTES